THE ESSENCE OF A CRIMSON HEART

The Essence of a Crimson

HEART

Expressing the Depth of Love, Nourishing the Soul and Ignite the Heart

Sophie A. Lille

Library of Congress Control Number: 2023923379

ISBN: 979-8-89228-015-0   (Paperback)
ISBN: 979-8-89228-017-4   (Hardcover)
ISBN: 979-8-89228-016-7   (eBook)

Printed in the United States of America

To the ones who color my world with love, passion, and all your support. Your presence is the essence of my crimson heart, inspiring every page of this book. With gratitude and love, my book The Essence of a Crimson Heart is dedicated to you.

Contents

ACKNOWLEDGEMENT

I extend my deepest gratitude to Atticus Publishing for their support and commitment to bringing this book to life. Special thanks to the Atticus Team, Bella, Ren, Rose, and Mathew for their expertise and guidance throughout the publishing process. This journey wouldn't have been possible.

HOLD ON

I found a way to make it through by holding on to you

Feeling stuck

The energy so thick

Tell me are you thinking of me

Cause I can't stop thinking of you

Losing control not able to move on

Drama is created

Believing with my whole heart
Although no guarantees in this life in space or time
Risk I shall take involving vulnerability and pain

NEVER THOUGHT I'D SEE THE DAY

The shadow before me

Can you hear me?

Can you tell me?

Needing a miracle today

Never thought I'd see the day you would leave me

You said we need to

Salvage what is left

Too old to fight

We've been down this road before

We know better

Putting our egos aside and our selfish needs to rest

Salvaging this friendship before we destroy what's left

Love is life
If you miss love
You miss life

SURVIVING THE FALL

Wanting to die
A profound unpleasant, intense sensory and emotional
agony I face
Falling is the beginning
A beginning to a new life
Came to realization
How beautiful
It is to be alive

I've cried in silence
For everything that has happened to me

Then you stop....
That's when you know you have survived the fall

UNDER IT ALL IS JUST FEAR

Strong I am
For how long?
Knowing the truth
Afraid of the unknown

Denial I face
With painful consequences
Closing the doors

Your body
A beautiful sculptured masterpiece
A fine piece of art indeed

OPEN HEART

I wouldn't be me if it weren't for you

My head up in the clouds
Feeling lost and alone
Then you appeared
Destined I suppose

My foggy mind is closed off and unclear
Afraid to be loved.
Afraid to love
Patience are unknown, but
You having them with me always

I wouldn't be me if it were not for you
Trust I'm having to build
Allowing me to open my heart

Being safe to trust you

Although still a long journey before me
Still not there yet

A few more mountains I have to climb
Make it known I will get to the other side
Facing the challenges I will stumble across
Never giving up
I hear your voice and encouragement embedded in my head

You my rock
Has always given me the strength in getting there

This being a promise to myself and to you
Wherever you are

Till we meet again....

SILENT VOICE

Can't move ahead
Reaching high, so high
My body paralyzed
A need to be heard

Fear of judgement
To be known as weak

Please comfort me
Help me release this fear and self-sabotaging

Feeling alone in my silence
Finding the courage
Taking a hold of the reins

Freeing myself of this self-imprisonment I have created

FOREVER

Something in your eyes
I see the reflection of you and me
I knew then I loved you and would from this day forward

Keeping my promise as I have to you
The hardest, the strongest love of all
I will always treasure you
A gift that was sent to me
A love that lasts forever
You and me

OBSERVATION

10

Sometimes surrender means giving up in understanding and
To become comfortable with the unknown

Remember standing in the fire
Strengthens the move
Going through it
Strengthens the mind

FALL IN LOVE WITH ONESELF

May be a cliché, but you
Must love oneself first

A pointer I may add...
Is the key to loving relationships

> *One who seeks enlightment*
> *Must be conscious of darkness*
> *By facing your own darkness*
> *Will you reclaim your freedom*

Rubics Cube

My mind
Soaks up information before me

Strategizing my every move
A mind of duality
With deep emotions and logic

Finding the balance within my soul
A tough task I must prevail

Concerning of people
An importance to win their trust

I silence the mind
As I find solace
My talented mind is off the grid at times

A quest
I master the art of meditation

The key to unlocking
The blockages

Branching and blossoming
I see through logical lens

Quieting the demons
From my mind as a child

Gods and monsters
Taunting my fears

I see the false evidence
Nothing stands in my way

Worked hard in silence

My heart is pure
With good intentions

I felt understood all my life
This being my journey and not anyone else's

I walk my own path
Not here to adhere to others

My soul yearns
In helping others

Seeing the outside world
Seeing conspiracies

Looking at facts
Finding truth
In making my own judgement
Allowing my mind and soul to shine, goal oriented to succeed.

STORED MIND

Building blocks of storage

A feeling of being off the scales at times
Powerful mind of overthinking
A need to shut down

Beliefs, corruption and even hatred
Still within me

Repressed emotions
Having fear is all

I then go into dream state
A place of solace
Finding love and empathy
A safe haven I possess

Soon back into reality
People in fear
Followers of corruption, lies and denial tendencies

Doing my best in coping
Doing my best not making judgement before them

Finding myself in a lonely space once again
A powerful mind with complexities and all the madness

A sense at times of not belonging in this strange world
Seeking for answers abroad
I must continue on my destined path

We don't age through maturity
We age with awareness

JOURNEY IMPORTANCE

As we get bored of day to day routine
A role we need to understand is

The journey plays more of an importance than the destination

The reason being,
The destination changes

Routine and consistency is needed to build it
Staying on course
To what you're building, not giving up and
Always thinking of thee final outcome

HOW TO SEE THE WORLD

I can't explain
How to see the world before me

A passage of time
Close your eyes
Lay still by my side
Feeling the earth slowly spinning around you

A galactic sphere
That's ever changing, sitting on its very axil

Visioning together to unknown places
Gliding through the Milky Way

Wise old souls we have become
Making the best of our path journey
As our time is limited

I ask you
What can we bring forth?

Helping others see through our visionary eyes through the
galaxy before us
A knowing as we have already seen

You're everything I have ever imagined
Is in my heart and soul

RECONCILED DIFFERENCES

Truth
Nothing but the truth

Truth will set us free

Having to heal the real truths and demons that lie within
Working on being a better person for myself and others,
from the deception put forth before me

Having healed the closure of you and me

Forgiveness I bring
To reconcile our differences

Timing being a factor

A lovely garden we have planted,
Nourishing it for growth

Both focusing on stability
Needing to communicate truthfully who we are, and what
we want

This relationship
Can stand the test of time

MISSING YOU

Wishing you were here

What a beautiful
Oasis in Desert Springs

A hot dry heat, not a cloud to be seen
Surrounded by sandy mountains, and very old palms of over
200 years

Embracing my every moment before me
With a beautiful picturesque of sunrises and sunsets in the
desert horizon

A place of tranquility
A stillness in space, I cannot even begin to express

A place I could call home
A place in the near future I foresee
To call a second home perhaps for you and me

A Cold Abyss

It's the only thing I hear

It's an emptiness of thought and of words

An abyss that accompanies me every single day and minute

I miss you....

WISHING YOU TIME

I only wish you what most people don't have

Wishing you time to enjoy and laugh

Wishing you time for you doing and thinking

Use it well, you will get something out of it but donate to others

Wishing you time, not to hurry or to run

Time to be happy not to just send but because you stayed

Wishing you time to find yourself to live your every day

It's a gift

Sophie A. Lille

LOVE DOESN'T HURT

Loneliness is painful
Rejection is painful
It hurts to lose someone

We get confused sometimes with the word, love hurts
Love is the only thing in the world that covers all the pain

STOP CHASING PERFECTION

Your "inner perfectionist" tells you that you're not good enough
It pushes to achieve more work harder and prove your worth

It tells you that the rest is lazy and hobbies are a waste of time
Perfectionism tells you that mistakes are castrophic and if
people see your flaws they'll reject or criticize you
So stop chasing perfection and feel good about who you are

CONTROL

People needing control over others
Is to make their unhappy souls feel empowered

No one should be controlling anyone
People are the only ones in control of themselves

UNIVERSE IS SPEAKING

Sometimes the universe has something to say
At times it forces us to make the changes that no longer
serve us
To our surprise it closes doors to force us to take another
direction to move us forward

The universe is a guide
It has a knowing we must trust

As circumstances arise out of nowhere to force us to make
the change
Some easier than others

We must trust the universe and not resist as it will lead us to
greater opportunities that will

Serve each and every one of us to a higher purpose and
not keep us where it does not serve
A place where we can grow in finding bliss and happiness

Teaching Our Children The Golden Rules Empowering Them Forever

Treat others as you want to be treated

Listen before speaking
Think before you speak
Be truthful
Be honest
Be grateful
Be kind? Never be selfish

This being the best gift and advice you could ever give
to a child

Thank you dad for teaching and reminding me of my
actions in making me the person I am today
Still embedded in my head space I share
Love to you

SOULS

Every waking part of my body
I'm reminded of you

My eyes open before me I see images of you
My smile in the mirror is a reflection of you
Every breath I take is the air we Share

Every beat of my heart
Beats yearning for you

The steps I walk meeting up with you...
For decade
This I cannot explain

Two souls connected that will never tear apart
Both of light and of darkness

We shine bright and fall in gloom

Staying in my power
This soon will pass

Taking a stand before me
Holding ones ground

True to my values
Even if met with disapproval

Express Ones Feelings

Feeling stuck in my head
It's all an illusion
My frustrations due to not having self-worth

I'm needing to love myself
Nurturing my mind, body and soul

A need to feel Im good enough as I was put here for a reason
It's my responsibility to put good use to those I serve and to
those who serve me

Life being a challenge before us all
One step in front of the other Walking many paths
Not sure of what cross road to take

The unknown taking a risk
Hoping this is not too turbulent
For it has brought me pain in the past

Pain we all have had
Some pain greater at different times

Needing to appreciate these pains
As it teaches us lessons
We must experience and grow in hope we learn and not
make them again

Scars we develop sometimes stick hard
Finding it hard to release because of the pain it caused

This is where it becomes a block that could cause more
pain in what is coming ahead into our future days
Preventing something truly amazing that we never thought
could ever be possible

Learning to love ourselves is much needed so we can pass
on our experiences of how important it is to not let life
challenges block who you are
That we are all worthy and put here for a purpose
Saying to ourselves daily
We are good enough

This will allow us to continue our journey and bring
abundance
Why?

Because you are good enough and you did the work
Being rewarded and for this you should be grateful and
it's perfectly ok to say
I love me

True Refection

You and I have conquered the stars
Live simple and let the storm pass us by

You and I
Have written the book line by line
The challenges it took to survive
Both yours and mine our loving hearts

If one of us shall go
Remember what I say today and forever
Of just how much I care and love you
I will always be there

One day you and I
Will show them the light we live by

Never again will they try
Try to keep us apart

Truth can never be taken away
Two people that have been brought together
Mirroring one another
Learning from their mistakes with pain and tribulations

Finding truth in oneself
A leader
Finding our purpose in helping others to find their truth
and happiness
In this world we see today

SET THE EXAMPLE

I will love you the exact way
I wanted to be loved

I Am Part Of Everything I Read

My curiosity leads me to books from all over the world
May they be old or new
With that unique book smell

Much knowledge from all over the world
May it teach and guide me to heighten my mind and
explore my greatest potential
On my journey before me

Emotions At War

Emotions rising whether
Past or present

A feeling of being overwhelmed
Cannot move forward if I cannot heal the pas

Giving oneself enough time to heal
Honoring yourself is at play

Emotions at war with heart and soul
Not making sense of it

When feeling unsettled within
A feeling in drowning Needing to come for air

Internal conflict
Not on even ground

I'm emotionally charged in my plans
With great challenges

Delays and setbacks
Being all part of the plan before me

Surrendering
Going with the flow trusting it will all work in my favor
Sometime being a blessing in disguise

I respect people who tell me the truth
No matter how hard it is to accept

A Precious Gift From Up Above

My guide
Watching and protecting over me
It was your light that helped and saved my very soul

This I'm so grateful and blessed
You still here
Having you by my side

I Am Not Afraid
Going into battle
Having strength that lies before me

Having much confidence
In speaking my truths and asserting my beliefs

Having no regrets
Now in my power, I must lead the way

CHECK IN

Thank you for giving me space
I'm in my head right now
I know what you want from me
Saddens me if you must know
The capacity just isn't there
Forcing myself staying out of my head
Pressure and anxiety building up
Too strong for me to cope, at this time

You cannot escape the lessons before you
You need to conquer them

LIFE GETS A BIT CRAZY

47

So you got a little crazy and distracted for awhile
That's perfectly ok

This being a tine to realign with your best self

Losing balance happens to best of us
Every day is a second chance

GUARDED LOVE

Sometimes it's a disadvantage to be so very guarded

If a woman can conceal her affection from the object of it

She may lose the opportunity of fixing him

Don't ever let the place you start, dictate where you finish

SILENCE

Not having much to say to me
A feeling of a lack of interest

You're completely mistaken
It has nothing to do with lack of interest
It has to do with their total interest in you

It's like when you see something that's beautiful
You go in a state of awwww
Lots for words just sitting and staring at it
Or when meeting someone that's feeds your soul, and not
having to even to speak to them
Feeling its, perfectly OK

Being in that space with them in pure silence
Yet still feeling the love around you and a feeling of being
safe

Let the silence be yours and embrace

Cycles In Life

In life we go through many cycles
Much like the 4 seasons

Some seasons better than others

Depends on what transitions we are going through in that
space and time
The challenging times...

Know it's a cycle and soon it will pass acceptance is needed

Believing with my whole heart, although no guarantees in
this life in space or time
Risk shall take involving vulnerability and pain

My Light

You came into my life your light so bright
Teaching me the game and the survival techniques
needed
In this life time

To stand strong
Keeping the little innocence
I still had left

Never ever wanting me to change
Never ever giving up

There were times
I had no fight left in me
Feeling very much alone
Wondering if this darkness would ever let up

You my love
Were put forth

We are all affected by external events

QUESTIONING ONES PATH

The fear of the unknown
Are we on the right path?

Doubt resurfacing
Using my intuitive gifts
Allowing new beginnings before me

LEAP OF FAITH

Take that leap with me
Going after our dreams as one
Let's make it happen...

Living with no regrets my love
Believing we can and we will

One step in front of the other
At a slow pace
Finding the balance
So I don't slip and fall

LIGHTHOUSE

Setting sail far away from here

Amongst the rough waters in darkness
I see a faint light amongst the fog before me

Allowing my sail to bring me to a safer place

Fighting through the raging wind that howls fiercely, battling
this horrific storm

Keeping my sail steady to calmer place

Approaching closer to shore
I see the lighthouse in the far distance

My anxiety lifting, drifting into shore
I know I have found my home

SOMEONE'S BURDENS

In life we can help alleviate
Struggles and burdens

Kindness is free giving, that warm fuzzy feeling we all need
time to time

You will be sure to make
Someone's day that much
More meaningful to them

Releasing Time you gave me being alone
Helped me to reflect on myself
What I don't have time for, but also realizing what
I do have time for

KEEPSAKE

♡ Powerful mind is everything

Remember ...

What you think you become

♡ First time I saw you I knew you were meant for me

♡ What is meant for you won't leave you it will be in your reach being your decision of wanting to purse or not

♡ Sometimes relationships separate us to help go within to grow and stay on our own journey that is meant for us all

♡ People only see what they confront

♡ Sometimes tangled the web we have weaved

♡ When we are in love with another it doesn't control nor does it possess it simply is an act of unconditional love

♡ How much are you really committed to yourself a test we have all had to face know we are

♡ Deserving of love

♡ Stay here with me against the world

♡ Look around you and me the moon the stars up above never feel alone in darkness together we bring the light the sun that shines today tomorrow and years to come

♡ A new beginning has entered my life do we choose to stay down once we have fallen

♡ One who seeks enlightenment must be conscious of darkness by facing your own darkness you will reclaim your freedom

♡ Love is the only thing we take with us it's we take from this life bringing into the next

♡ Stepping up to the challenges before me

♡ Freeing my past wounds healing scars deep within allows me to move forward towards my desired dreams

♡ You not get a second chance to make a first impression

♡ Best friends and lovers support one another's dreams growing together on different levels

♡ Inspiring one another's interest which can eventually build a solid bond between two